MY FIRST LEARNING SERIES
ADDING

Written and Illustrated by Caroline and John Astrop

Text and illustrations ©1993 by Caroline and John Astrop.
Originally published by Regency House Limited.

Modern Publishing
A Division of Unisystems, Inc./New York, New York 10022
Printed in the U.S.A.

Mama Duck has two babies
and only one orange.
How many more oranges does she have to buy?

Which basket has two things in it?

**Two birds on a branch.
If one more bird comes to join them,
how many will there be on the branch?**

**How many more hats do we need
so that each frog has one?**

Two red cars and two blue cars.
How many cars are there altogether?

**Three pink fish and one yellow fish.
How many fish are in the bowl?**

**Three sad bears and two happy bears.
How many bears are there?**

Which square has five candies?

**Four flowers on one hat,
two flowers on the other.
How many flowers altogether?**

How many more clothespins do we need
to hang the rest of the socks?

**One flower has four leaves
and the other has three.
How many leaves altogether?**

4 + 3 = 7

**Pig wants seven apples in his basket.
How many more must he pick?**

**Spider has only four shoes.
How many more does he need?**

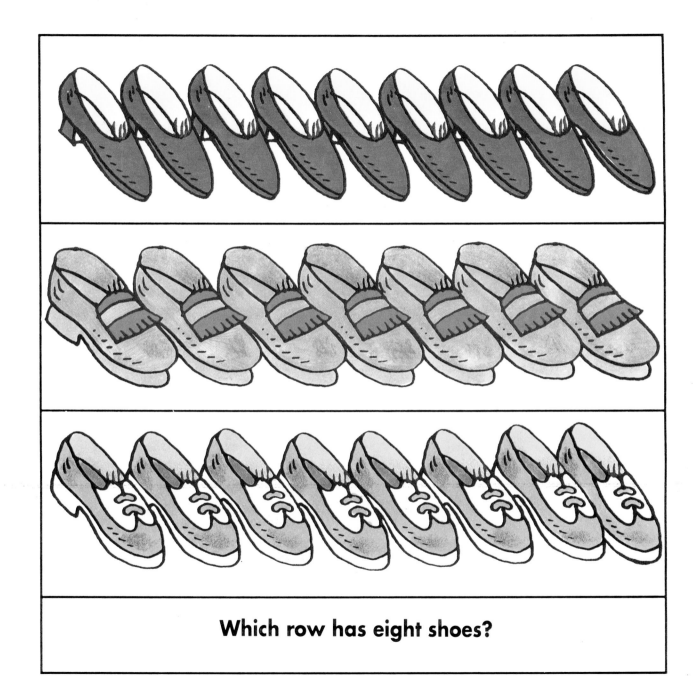

Which row has eight shoes?

Five red balloons and four orange ones.
How many balloons altogether?

Mama hen can see six chicks.
How many more make nine?

Five butterflies and five bees.
How many insects altogether?

$$5 + 5 = 10$$

Ten dolls only have five chairs.
How many more do they need?

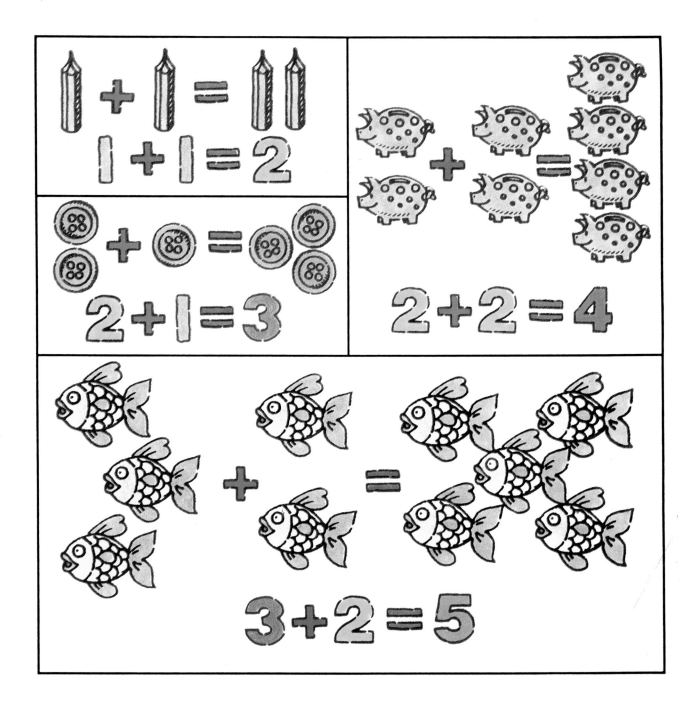

4 + 2 = 6

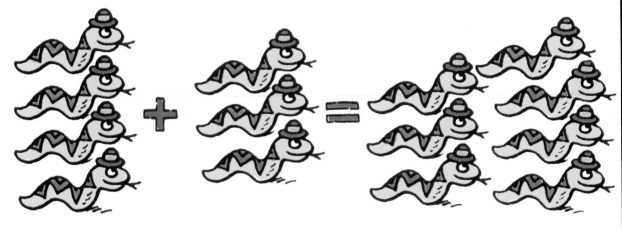

4 + 3 = 7

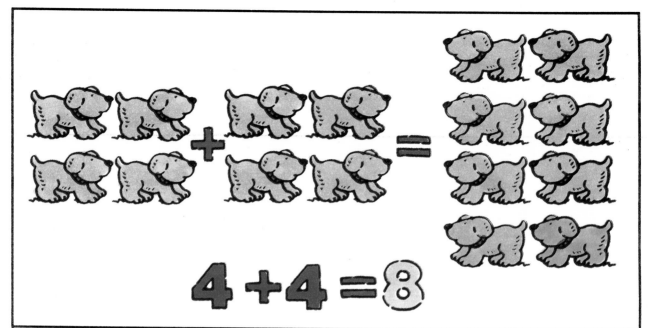

4 + 4 = 8

5 + 4 = 9

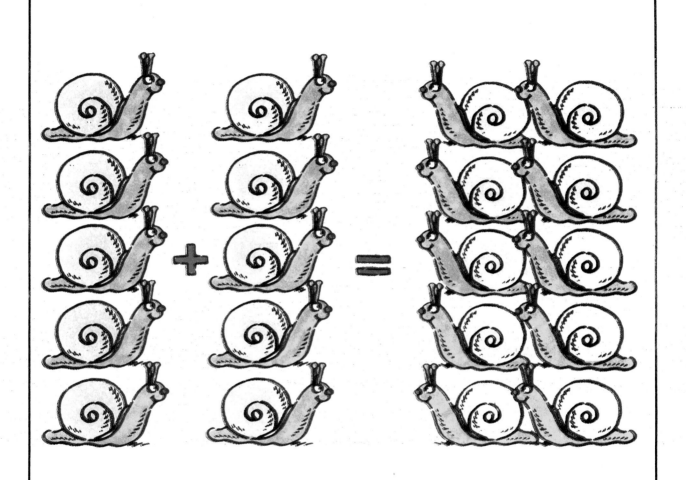

5 + 5 = 10

We hope you
enjoyed learning
about

ADDING